Saved, Single, Selibate ...
and waiting on God

Anita +
Praise God for
Miss Bea. (Your God-Mother)

May God Continue to Bless You!

Sis. A. Stephens -

TABLE OF CONTENTS

Please note all scripture was taken from the Life Application Bible, King James Version, unless noted otherwise

ACKNOWLEDGEMENTS

First I would like to thank God for providing the vision to write this book. I could have never completed this work without the help of the Holy Spirit, I love you. I thank God for my Mother, Elder Dolores J. Shepherd, my family and my dear friends (who are also my family). My editor, Linda Wright of Wright Communications, I thank God for you, and your beautiful gift of effective communicating. I believe it's the relationships in our lives that assist God in shaping who we are, and who we will become, in the future. And to you, the reader, I thank you for taking the time to read this book, you will be blessed.

AUTHOR'S NOTE

Habakkuk chapter 2, verse 2

"And the Lord answered me, and said, Write the vision, and make it plain upon tables, that he may run that readeth it."

My sister, this book that you behold is just one of the 1,000,000 copies that will be printed and read. And, with aid from the Holy Spirit, I know this book will bless your life and your walk with God. I love you, dearly.

Chapter 1
My Promise to God

Lisa A. Shepherd, July 9, 1993

"God please forgive me of my sin, I promise you that I will not sleep with another man until you bless me with my husband, please forgive me."

I was a virgin until the age of 25. And, 25 was my most favorable and heart felt year. I also rededicated my life to God, accepting my Savior, Jesus Christ as Lord, at the age of 25, at The Oakley Full Gospel Baptist Church. I graduated from college, and I lost my great-grandmother, Annie Mae Livingston, who was like a second mother to me, all at the age of 25. We love us some grandma's huh? My Grams was the second parent I never had. My mother, Elder Dolores J. Shepherd, was a single, wonderful, understanding, selfless parent to me, my two older brothers, Timothy and Nicholas (daughter Erica) and my older sister Lea, (son, Bobby, daughters, Brittany and Brandi).

Grams was 96 years old when she went to heaven, and every last one of her grandchildren, great grandchildren and great-great grandchildren loved this women fiercely. Grams

1

was one of those grandmothers, (like most African American grandmothers) who had to sacrifice her life's goals, and her formal education for the sake of her children. Grams never had the privilege to experience the concept of the ABC's. My beloved was completely illiterate. But, she was the smartest person I have ever known. And I loved this woman who could make a pound cake (called sweet bread) from memory.

Grams would insist that we go and pick our own switch from the tree in the back yard, and the same switch would leave whelps for disobedience, all for the sake of love. The same woman would tend her garden as if it were part of the first sacred garden, and she would also iron every article of clothing. Before my grandfather, (my mother's father, and Gram's son, William Hardrick) passed away he told my great grandmother that I would be there to take care of her, and her needs.

2

You see, when my mother went on vacations, my sister, Lea would beg and plead to go stay with my mother's older sister, Pauline, and her children: Jimmy, Ruth Anne (First Lady of Emmanuel Apostolic Missionary Church), Tonya, Laurie and William. My brothers would request to stay with my Mother's younger sister, Pastor Clarice Burger, (Pastor of God's House of Restoration Chosen Generation) and her boys, Tony, Rob, and Gene, her husband, and Co-Pastor.

I wanted to stay with my great grandmother, always. Sometimes I would stay with my grandmother's niece, Josie Mae, and her two older daughters, Diana and Margaret. I never wanted to run the streets with my sister and cousins. I wanted to stay home, to hear my great grandmother's stories on how cotton is planted and picked. As I look back over my life, I can see the work of God, shaping my life.

The desire I had to stay with my great grandmother was the foundation that kept me out of trouble, and drug free to this day, praise God. So, when my grandfather died, I took the responsibility of caring for my great grandmother, thus eliminating my aspiration of attending college out of state. I remember, how I would tell everyone, "I am taking care of my great grandmother. I take her to the store, bank and the doctor's office, and I take her to pay her bills."

God blessed me, and I was not even aware of the magnitude and the impact of the 12 years God gave me to care for my Grams. The situation was really completely opposite. It was my great grandmother who took care of me! Daily, she would kindly instruct me in very subtle ways how to be a lady, how to be a God fearing Christian *and how to be a person who must treat everyone in the same manner as I would want to be treated. Grams knew the scriptures as well as the local pastor and she attended The Mount Vernon African Methodist Church. God was molding and shaping me, and He allowed my great grandmother to live as long as she lived, for me, (and my entire family) and I am so very thankful. To have a grandparent like my Grams is to have a real and solid blessing from God.*

I had one boyfriend all through junior and senior high school, but when I did not marry him after high school he dumped me, for the life of me, I cannot remember shedding one tear. I was semi-popular during high school, and most of the popularity came from my older brothers and sister; and the fact that I played sports, all year round, tennis, basketball and softball. After my high school sweetheart dumped me, (thanks Jay!)

guys started popping up. I began to date all types of men, and I was totally partial to older men. I love a man who truly knows how to treat a woman, and what I mean by that is this: Brothers, please open the door for a lady, and please do not walk in front of a lady, (unless you are holding her hand, guiding her along). If you walk in front, you will miss any trouble she may be stumped by, because your back is to her. If you are walking behind or at her side, you will have all bases covered.

I truly believe that song is so true. A real man knows a real woman when he sees her. You all know what I am talking about, the kind of man that is comfortable with a single woman without children, an education, independent but, dependent on God.

I would love a man who knows all about the concepts of compromise, positive submission, (on my end) and constructive criticism, a strong man who fears God; the kind of man who loves and respects his mother, sisters, aunts and grandmothers. I'm talking about a man who would not mind cutting my meat, or buttering my bread during dinner, and he would allow the night to be "Dutch" without feeling threatened. He would be a man who would love and cherish my love for him. Most of all, I would be so very thankful if God blessed me with a man who was brave and secure enough to call me, beautiful, Mercy! One of my heart's desires is to marry a gentleman of God.

Proverbs chapter 18, verse 22

"Whoso findeth a wife findeth a good thing, and obtaineth favour of the Lord."

This scripture shows us that the word of God approves of marriage as a joyful and good creation of God. God created marriage, and my *sisters, if your desire is as strong as mine to be married, it's OK. There is nothing wrong with you or that desire. There is nothing wrong with wanting to be married, and we must not allow society (friends, family members, etc) to place the single women in a box, labeling us as desperate women.*

I had an associate, Kim, call me desperate. She said, "Lisa, I told my fiancé about you and I told him how desperate you were to be married." I smiled at Kim, and explained to her that I was desperate for God's favor, and no more. As women of God, we must not allow society to label us. I am sure you all are aware of that old saying, "you are what you think you are." And, if you begin to believe what your associates say about you, you will not ever progress forward.

I once told my entire book club, that I was very beautiful, and blessed by God. At the next meeting, one of the sisters stated, that I was very beautiful, and blessed. You see, I told these women what to think and what to believe about Lisa, and trust me, they were all good thoughts.

The man I described earlier, "a gentleman of God," also has God's favor. He is a wise man, because he has obeyed God and His commandments, thus trying to live right. My sisters, just think how wonderful and positive life will be when God blesses you with a man who has favor with Him. I thank you right now, Father, and I love you. Sisters, it's OK if one of your heart's desires is to be married. God created marriage.

My sisters, I dated many men who, if I combined several qualities from each man, I could tally up these attributes, and have one good man. I was blessed to find one man who came close, all by himself, with no outside help, when I was 25.

This brother loved his mother, and they were the best of friends. And his mother was very determined to "mold" her only child into a "good" man.

This brother was a young girl's dream my dream, come true. The first time I met this brother he told me, "You have beautiful lips" and he licked his, in the same manner as LL Cool J does on stage, teasingly. I was speechless. I was also young and impressionable. If the brother had told me he was really Denzel Washington, I would have believed that too, smile.

Although I am old fashion, I feel it's the brother's responsibility to ask for my number first, I asked him for his telephone number. This was the first time that I had ever asked for a guy's telephone number, but I was so caught up by this man, protocol was the last thing on my mind. Our first date was within the week, I was totally

smitten. *My sisters, I am sure you will all agree
that there is nothing like a nice man with a friendly
personality and kind disposition.*

Proverbs chapter 22, verse 6

*"Train a child in the way he should go, and when
he is old he will not turn from it."*

*The brother I'm talking about loved and respected
his mother fervently. There would be special times,
when the three of us would be together and his
mother would constantly check him on his values
and morals, without demeaning his manhood. The
sister was so cool, that she would educate her son,
instruct him on how to treat a lady, and love would
overflow from every step she took in "training"
her only child.*

    *Ladies, we know that our parents help set
our morals and our overall character at an early
age in life. As we grow into adulthood, society*

(associates, friends, co-workers, personal relationships, college and family) can alter our disposition in positive and negative areas.

I praise God my mother raised me with high moral standards. Praise God, with my mother's positive style of child rearing, I was destined to attract similar people, men and women, into my life. If someone is training you, (train up a child) they are dedicated to you and your life. I love more, and I smile more, when I seek the kingdom of God daily, by having conversations with Him.

I want peace in my life, so I try to avoid conflict and stress at all times. I want and seek happiness daily. I desire more from God, and the Holy Spirit is showing/training me how I should live, according to God's word. Via another relationship in my life, I can see the hand of God shaping me. This brother's mother taught me a lesson: Instruction and discipline at all times, is the best way to "train up a child."

I praise God, I am His child, and as God reshapes my life and heart, into what He would have me become, I know that I will never settle for just any man. I will wait on God. This brother and I dated and were lovers for three months. But, because God had His hand in the pot, our break up was not as hard on me as I thought it would be.

I knew the entire time I dated this man, that our sex life was wrong. The physical feelings I experienced were "the bomb" but within my heart, I knew something was wrong. God was convicting me, but I was clueless as to what conviction was, mentally and physically, and I did not understand how to act on His conviction. I believe that God always has a plan. Although I lost my virginity at 25, I began another type of physicality, too, Christianity.

2 Corinthians chapter 5, verse 17

"Therefore, if anyone is in Christ, he is a new creation: the old has gone, the new has come!"

Inside, my heart had changed, and I had no clue what was happening to me. My sisters, this is how God will bless you sometimes, without your total awareness, thank you Jesus. Once you confess with your mouth, and believe in your heart that Jesus Christ is Lord, you become united with Jesus through faith in Him. And a commitment to Him will become your life's aspiration.

Once I confessed that Jesus was my Lord and Savior, a restoration began to take place which cleared the muddy water, my life; and lead me toward a fulfillment in wanting to live "right" according to God's word, and His commandments.

I continued to date, but I kept my legs closed. I recalled the feelings I had after sex, and I did not want to experience those same emotions. I know now they were God's conviction, but at that time, I was unsure of where the feelings were coming from, and their meaning. Six months before my 27th birthday, I began dating an older man. For my birthday we went on a weekend trip, to a Bed and Breakfast. We planned to return from the weekend early Sunday morning, which happened to be my birthday.

That Sunday morning, in church, I was very sick in my stomach and my heart was heavy. It felt as though someone I loved had died. I remember my head was pounding as if I had been beat up in a fight. My hands were sweaty, I felt nauseated, my ears were plugged, and I was hurting. It was the conviction of God. I knew that I was wrong, and that what I had done over the weekend was not right, and very disrespectful, to God.

In church, during the season of praise and worship, God spoke to me, and He told me that I was wrong, and that I had sinned against Him, and that I had to cease right away. He did not go into detail, or say any names, or point out my precise sin. He simply said that I had to stop. I knew exactly what He was referring to, sex.

I knew having sex outside of marriage was wrong from the very first time, at the age of 25. My conviction was mentally suffocating me, while the new creation in me was battling for my soul. The Holy Spirit was teaching me how to understand God's conviction, and most of all how to act on my feelings from the conviction. My next step was to repent (confess my sins) and not go back to them, and to move forward in Christ Jesus.

I was now able to connect the foreign feelings to my thoughts and then to my Father's wishes. I began to pray, "God, please forgive me of my sin, I promise you that I will not sleep with another man until you bless me with my husband, please forgive me." God continued molding my life, and through this event I moved to a higher level in Him. I praise God for keeping me safe and caring for me, loving me, and most of all, for second chances.

1 John chapter 1, verse 9

"If we confess our sins, he is faithful and just and will forgive us our sins and purify us from all unrighteousness."

God wants to forgive us. He allowed His precious son Jesus to die for us, so He could pardon us from our sins. My confession cleared my blurred path to God. The path had been muddled, from my blatant sin against God. Confession opened up the airways to a better fellowship with God. Please note, true confession from the heart means that I

17

had to turn away from the sin. God is so awesome once you confess your sin, there is no need to continue to confess that sin, over and over, God will wipe your slate clean. Praise Him!

After my promise to God, I dropped to my knees and began to praise God, because the heaviness was no longer in my heart. God is so awesome. He will forgive us that easily. The Lord began to show me through His word how sinful and dirty this act (sex outside of marriage) is to the Christian life.

I know you all are wondering why I chose to spell the word celibacy as "selibacy." I was instructed by the Holy Spirit to spell it that way. When God blessed me with the vision to write this book, He also gave me the title, the outline and the structure of the book. I was also directed to go on a fast every time I sat down to write this book, thus allowing the Holy Spirit to totally lead.

Side Bar:

My sisters, I truly did not want to write this book. I simply wanted God to bless me with the desires of my heart. I was not a happy person regarding this task. I did not want to take on another challenge, work or duty. I continued to pray, and ask God, "please, look beyond me and please bless me anyway, please." My Father (I know He was giving me a half smile) told me to stop complaining, and not to go forward another day saying what I do not want to do for Him. I repented.

In Webster's dictionary, the phrase right next to a word (usually in parentheses and in italics) instructs the reader how to correctly pronounce the word. The phrase next to celibacy was spelled (sel e be se). You all have to believe that I was grinning hard. To be sure, I asked our Father about the spelling of the word. He laid it on my heart to look the word up in the dictionary, and there was a phrase spelled the same way God had instructed me to spell it, I knew this mission was of God. Please note that I am not trying to insult anyone's intelligence. The definition of celibacy is "complete sexual abstinence," complete meaning totally, 100 percent without something you may desire.

I praise God that this promise I made Him was somewhat easy for me, all due to His molding of my heart through His conviction. My promise to God became very personal, so I did not want to share the promise I made to God with anyone. I felt that the promise was between Him and me, our secret. Although I dated, I had no problem abstaining; abstaining was my promise to God, plain and simple. Have you ever made a promise to God? The Christian life can sometimes be one-sided, God offering promises and we, His children

20

reaping the benefits. And sometimes we are so undeserving, or should I speak only for myself?

Chapter 2

The Desires of My Heart

Psalms chapter 37, verse 4

"Delight thyself also in the Lord; and he shall give thee the desires of thine heart."

God has truly blessed me, through His molding of my heart. I began to love more, and my disposition was open to receive love from others, both giving and taking love unconditionally. I can only praise God, because I know that it was not my hand, but His, thank you Jesus! He showed me how to love myself first, on a deeper level.

First, God showed me what I really looked like, and once I saw how ugly and vain I was, I began to ask God to renew my heart, my mind and my spirit, so that I could shine for Him. One tool God used to mold my heart was my wonderful mother. My Mother provided me and my brothers and sister with an abundance of love. And, through the stacks of love she supplied, and with God's help, I began to see myself in a different light, and, I began to truly love Lisa.

Dating before I turned 30 was wonderful. The men I dated treated me like a lady, doors opened, no cussing. God blessed me to date "nice" guys. Through the love I had for myself, I was able to use the gift of discernment, (distinguishing between what is true and what could possibly be a falsehood), when selecting men to date. Are you wondering why I never chose one of the "nice" guys to marry? I was waiting on God. I am still waiting on God. I knew in my heart that when I met him, it was going to be love at first sight or fireworks.

I also believed that God would totally confirm the relationship. And, while dating, I never found the love at first sight, the fireworks nor God's confirmation. I was looking for one or all three in every man I dated.

I was getting tired, mentally, of waiting on God to bless my life (I am simply keeping it real.) And I developed a huge complex over the fact that I was over the age of thirty, and single with no children. I am sure you all are aware of how family, friends and society will treat a saved, beautiful, independent, intelligent (all by the grace of God) woman with dreams...not good at all.

Sooooo, after the age of 30, I quit dating "unsaved" men, because I figured that I must be doing something wrong. I asked God... "Lord, I am still waiting. Please tell me what I am doing wrong, or better yet, what I have done wrong, so I can repent, and I pray that you will bless me, soon, please?" Needless to say, after my declaration of no more "unsaved" men was out, I was dateless for at least two years. You all know I owned that "woe is me" line. No date, no boyfriend, meant no couple parties, no holding hands while walking in the park, no strong arms to hold me when I needed it, no kissing, no heavy flirting, nothing.

Emotions were bestowed upon me like someone would receive traits like dimples, freckles or a pretty smile, but I was unable to act on my emotions. And God withheld one of my greatest requests, love. You see, I have always been an affectionate person; I am a person who loves to distribute hugs and kisses to people, especially my family, my close friends, and my church family.

I have always felt in my heart that God blessed me with the gift of love. I simply wanted love from a man, a man predestined just for me and my life, so that my life may be blessed with children. Since the age of 16, I have wanted a baby. I have been waiting for 20 years for God to bless me with this desire of my heart. It's like wanting something, all your life and you move closer to that desire by improving your life's standards on a spiritual level by accepting Jesus Christ as your personal Savior, but, things become worse instead of improving.

Most people may laugh at me, or shake their heads at one of my greatest desires, love. But, my reality, my plight, my issues and desires are very important, to me, they are the air that I want to breathe for my future. I know that I cannot make my own decisions. Although I have a choice, I must always choose God. His decision far outweighs mine for my life, I truly believe that. We all tend to down play other people's struggles. But it's not fair, because we all handle our plight in life differently, and our common bond is that we must trust in God.

I can remember having several conversations with sisters who happened to be married with kids, regarding my plight. I explained, in detail the struggle regarding my single hood at the age of 35. Most of these women tisked over my plight, and replied..."Girl you are the blessed one. You say you want a husband and kids, but trust me, no you don't. I wish that I were in your shoes. You have no idea how lucky you got it. Girl you have your freedom." This was a very common response. They say that the grass is greener on the other side, but on my side I was only working with dirt. I would bet my hair on the fact that those sisters who are married to "saved" men thank God daily.

Can you believe their response to my plight? It would be like my downplaying a sister who is strung out on drugs, because the thorn in my side is completely different from the thorn in the side of the sister on crack. I nod my head, point my finger and tell her to get over her addiction.

By doing that I would be totally disregarding the profound nature of this sister's plight, because it's not the same trial or tribulation that I am experiencing. Because I am drug free, I assume being drug free is easy for everyone.

I could never speak on what life is like for a crack addict, nor could married women with children speak on or against my life, being single and childless at the age of 35.

I wish for each one of these sisters to be given the opportunity to walk in my shoes. My sisters, they could never handle it! Within my state: single, unmarried and childless after 30, I was tripping big-time. I prayed and prayed to God. I fasted, and I stayed in scriptures week after week, month after month and year after year. Nothing changed. I once heard a Pastor preach on writing your vision down on paper. "Make it plain, describe what you want to God, and tell Him all about it." I wrote down my heart's desires, and I began to pray, and ask God for help.

I deeply felt that God had molded my heart and my thought process. The desires that I listed subconsciously stemmed from God. The primary desire I focused on was having children, and the remaining desires branched off from my need to have a family. I believed that God placed the desires in my heart, and through His love for me, I knew that my desires would come to fruition. This idea was the sole piece of thread I had to hold onto. It was my hope. God loves me, right? After years of waiting and watching most of my friends, family and associates receive their heart's desires, I began to wonder if God really loved me.

My circle of friends and family were receiving their heart's desires. We all were trying to achieve the same goal, loving God with our total heart, and trying to live "right," realizing it's our reasonable service to God. Their blessings continued to flow, and I continued to praise God with my family and friends for their blessings. God loves me, too, right? The feelings within my heart regarding God's lack of love for me, took me *on a mental journey that I am still trying to overcome.*

The list of my desires is still in my planner. I was so confused, you see God blessed me with a heart to love enormously, yet He never gave me an Adam to love. I felt that this deed was the worst possible state for my life. It was a mental suffering that I was experiencing, a type of distress that I would never wish on anyone.

God is so amazing. You see, He was still using me to do His work, and I was still in His will. But, in my personal life I felt like I was sinking in quick sand. And God had allowed more and more trials and tribulations to come along and step on my head, thus pushing me closer to the death of self.

Nevertheless I was still in His will, on a spiritual level God was moving me to higher levels in Him: He began to heal people through me, He increased my ability within discernment, and God used me to witness to my friends, and their friends, thus saving souls for Him. God also developed and organized my already joyful and positive disposition. He blessed me with a heart to love and a spirit to give.

I became a listener and most of all He strengthened my idealist state of mind. You see, I am a dreamer, and a person filled with hope. The ideas and dreams I see and wish upon, I actually believe they will come true. God was molding me, even in my state of distress.

Job chapter 6, verse 8

"Oh that I might have my request; and that God would grant me the thing that I long for!"

Job wanted to give in, to be freed from his suffering, and to die. Although my life is not on the same level as Job, I can sympathize with the man that had one of the greatest tests in the Bible. I too, would love for God to grant me one of the things I long for, one of the desires of my heart. I believe this blessing will assist in keeping my hope alive.

I know it was wrong to equate physical blessing to God's love, but my reality was very much real and in my face, daily. After a fast, the Holy Spirit blessed me to be in the congregation of a Pastor who preached about the love of God. His scripture came from:

Isaiah chapter 41, verse 10

"Fear thou not; for I am with thee: be not dismayed; for I am thy God: I will strengthen thee; yea, I will help thee; yea, I will uphold thee with the right hand of my righteousness."

My sisters, when times are bad, and your heart feels heavy, I urge you to call on the Holy Spirit,

He will help you, trust me. I remember during this time in my life, I wanted to give up; I wanted to go out and have fun. I wanted more happiness in my life. God blessed me. He laid it on my heart to fast more, pray more, and attend Bible study with the saints of God.

I pressed on toward a fellowship of people worshipping and praising God on a week day. God does love me, and He loves you, too. We must not ever forget this, He is faithful and righteous, the beginning and the end, and He knows what is best for our lives. We must trust in God, and if we ever have issues on God's love for us, we must pray and ask the Holy Spirit to help and guide us. He will bless you, as He blessed me.

My sisters, I felt that God loved me but life was not getting any better for me. All of my sister-girlfriends had men. And, some of my girlfriends were married, and most of them had children. I was single and waiting on God, I felt as if I were bringing up the rear. I have a small circle of friends consisting of Patti, Diana, Dionne, Coco, Ching-Yi and Monica. Patti, who has been my friend for over 12 years, is like my older sister. She is married to Steve and has two boys, Steven and Kyle. God has blessed Patti with an abundance of wisdom and I thank God for Patti. Diana, who has been my friend for over 15 years, is my Apostolic, no pants wearing, Holy Ghost filled, spiritual sister, and she is married to Jeff, and has two kids, Terrell and baby Olivia.

Dionne, who has been my friend for over 15 years, is my sister-girlfriend who has three beautiful kids: Tony, Alexis (my god-daughter) and Shayla; Dionne and I should have been twins, we are so much alike, friendly and very loving. Coco, who has been my friend for over 28 years, is my little spiritual sister, filled with the Holy Ghost.

She is married to Corie, with a son, C.J. (Corie Jr.) and she is currently pregnant with her baby girl. Ching-Yi, my Asian-American sister-girlfriend for three years, who will be a doctor soon, (The Ohio State University Doctorate in Pharmacy program) praise God, Ching! The last sister within my circle of friends is Monica, and she is my best friend. Monica attends Oakley, too, and, God blessed me with two god-sons, Cameron and Joshua.

I was single but I never lacked for love. My family and friends truly blessed me. My mother is one of my greatest blessings. My mother, bless her heart, had four babies by the age of 22. My mother was a middle child, and she has always felt left out of many things in life, including love. Like most single parents, my mother worked very hard. She worked 12-hour shifts, and raised her children the best she could. We never wanted for anything.

God truly blessed me and my brothers and sister, by giving us Mommy. I feel extra blessed because I live with Mom. Mom had a mastectomy when I was in junior high school, thus weakening her entire left side.

Ten years later the cancer returned, in one of her lungs. She had the tumor cut off her lung, thus leaving her lung damaged, and she suffers from shortness of breath, if she overexerts herself. Five years later, the oncologist found three tumors, in her midsection. On my 33rd birthday the oncologist looked me in the eye and said... "Your mother will have only six months to live." Two and one half years later, my mother is alive and healed. I thank God for his healing power. Mom was also diagnosed with arthritis in her back, and diabetes. I thank God for one of my greatest blessings, my mother.

In the area of my heart's desires, it was as if I were asking for so little, and receiving nothing. On top of the fact that I was 35 and I was still single and childless, I was also jobless. I had graduated from college at the age of 25, and I had been looking for a job since graduation. I had been working a part-time job for five years and I also worked for several temporary agencies. I applied for several positions that I was under and over qualified for, and I received no employment. I had a system regarding applications for the city, state and county government; and there were specific days of the week I would hit the pavement looking for employment within the private sector.

In the midst of this trial I had to deal with a $30,000 debt from college, and stay afloat on my remaining bills, all were paid with a part-time job and with the assistance of my mother. My mother allowed me to live rent-free, I thank God.

Although I am still in debt, I have to believe that through my faithfulness of tithing, God will bless me in this area, too.

I truly believe that the heart is the center of the human spirit, and your emotions, your thought process, motivations and feelings come from this wellspring of life. When we delight ourselves, our thoughts and our emotions in God, and commit to this very act, there is no way we can go wrong in life. Once we make this commitment to God, we trust God for everything. While writing this book, I really, really, wanted more from God. I wanted more of His anointing, more understanding, on why I am single at the age of 35, and more wisdom, in how to handle my current state.

At one of my Interdenominational Christian Women's Fellowship meetings, Von Thomas Ministries, one of the evangelists repeated this phrase over and over again, "every round goes higher and higher." I knew there was a lesson within that saying for me, because this lady was really working my nerves. She kept repeating it over and over, but she would not explain what she meant by her words.

I asked the Holy Spirit for help. The Holy Spirit showed me that every trial and tribulation you experience is a round. And once you receive victory (by overcoming the trial or tribulation, with the help of God) you move higher and higher in the Lord. The grin on my face was enormous. Everything I go through in life, every trial and tribulation, God helps me to get over the hurdle and moves me closer (higher) to Him, in my spiritual journey. God is wonderful!

Chapter 3
My Little Sister, From God, Coco

Proverbs chapter 17, verse 17(a)

"A friend loves at all times"

When I was 8 years old, my mother moved from the HillTop in Columbus, Ohio, and purchased our first new home, further up the hill in a community called "Alice Rita." Just a few weeks after the relocation our first neighbors moved in right next door. As I waited patiently outside, hoping to get a glimpse of the boys and girls who were moving in. One petite little girl came outside to play.

Her name was Coco, and she was only three years old. Coco had one brother, Tyrone, and I love Ty as much as I love Tim and Nick, my biological brothers. Coco and I smiled at each other, and began to play, and from that date on, Coco and I have been the greatest of friends. We played kick ball, jumped to our own tunes in Double-Dutch, played flag football, basketball, cheerleading, four square and curb ball, we also made mud pies, played in the creek in the backyard and played many more games we made up.

To help explain my and Coco's history, she was my shadow, plain and simple, a friend who has been in my life for more than 28 years. The most amazing aspect of our relationship is that Coco and I love and trust each other, unconditionally, just like sisters. I thank and praise God for my biological sister, Lea. She is a blessing, and I love her with all my heart. Lea and my two brothers love and spoil me madly. I am blessed.

I am grinning thinking of my little sister, Coco. She is a blessing to my life. Coco is the younger sister I never had, and she respects my opinion, and listens to my advice, even if it is unwanted, and loves me completely. As close friends, Coco and I experienced the different stages sisters progress through. For instance the first time I carried a purse, Coco wanted one.

When I was able to wear high heals, Coco had to have a pair, too. And when my mother allowed me to stay out longer, Coco desired the same. She would often ask to spend the night at my house, (where she was able to stay on the telephone past 10pm, because my mother was cool. She did not do "phone checks" throughout the night.) While spending the night, she would see me off to the football game and welcome me home from the dance, waiting to hear about all the excitement of a 16-year-old.

Coco followed me through most of my stages in life, like: wearing makeup (lipstick and mascara only) and the ups and downs of being a teenager, having a boyfriend and being a cheerleader, (Coco was the mascot.)

As neighbors and friends, I, Coco, Tyrone, the kids on the block shared everything from cookies to bikes. We were all great friends.

I can remember when Coco's younger sister, Christina, was born. Coco was so excited she finally had a younger sister and she would now be able to play the big sister role. Christina's birth placed Coco as a middle child and all the cons that go hand in hand with being a middle child were thrust upon Coco. Thus our relationship grew stronger.

With the blessings of youth, we never thought about our relationship, asking ourselves which was the taker and who gave more. We simply included one another in our lives, like sisters. I was her listening ear. She came to me with her problems and concerns, because she knew I would listen, and that I would seek to do whatever I could to make her situation and life easier. As I look back over our relationship, I can see how God kept us both, and blessed our relationship. I believe that God predestined our friendship, and I thank Him daily.

When Coco was 24, God delivered her out of a relationship with a man who had been selling drugs, sleeping around on her, and having babies outside of their relationship. She was also living with this guy, too. Coco chose this path to get away from home, but after her deliverance, she returned home. When Coco came back home, I was 29, and I had rededicated my life to God. I was living for Him, trusting, hoping and waiting on God for my future.

Coco obtained a cosmetology license, while living with her boyfriend, and when she came back home, she began to do hair in her mother's basement. And because I received my roller-sets, "relaxers" and wraps free, I began to visit Coco's beauty salon weekly.

Our bonding within the salon magnified, due to God's blessings in my spiritual life, and the work of the Holy Spirit who blessed me to be a witness to Coco, on a weekly basis. I remember she once called our sessions her Bible study. One thing I must mention about Coco, a most favorable asset in her life, is that God has blessed her with an obedient heart.

With the help of the Holy Spirit, I explained to Coco what was going on in my life, and how I had rededicated my life to Christ at the age of 25. The Holy Spirit was truly working on me, and my life. He was teaching me how to witness to Coco, without talking too much, or being judgmental. I began to explain to Coco my promise to God and the relationships I experienced that had played a key part in my life.

45

God was molding me, again, and I had no clue. I simply thought that I was having a conversation with a friend. I simply was sharing how wonderful God is, and how He will forgive us of our sins. Together, Coco and I went over the Ten Commandments, **Exodus, chapter20**, *in order to find out which one (or two, or three) of God's laws we were failing to live up to, in life. Please remember, Coco's disposition. She has the gift of obedience. If she literally viewed God's word, and found in her heart she was sinning against God, Coco would cease all negative activity.*

I can remember Coco saying, "You know I would not ever steal. It says in the Bible, 'Thou shall not steal,' and I will not steal. It would go against what God wants, and I am afraid of God." The Holy Spirit blessed me to show Coco another scripture. I knew this scripture would move Coco's heart to come back to God, and rededicate

*her life to Jesus Christ (she was baptized at the
age of 10).*

1 Corinthians chapter 11, verses 23 – 25

*23. "For I have received of the Lord that which
also I delivered unto you, That the Lord Jesus the
same night in which he was betrayed took bread:
(24) And when he had given thanks, he brake it,
and said, Take, eat: this is my body, which is
broken for you: this do in remembrance of me. (25)
After the same manner also he took the cup, when
he had supped, saying, This cup is the new
testament in my blood: this do ye, as oft as ye drink
it, in remembrance of me."*

*Jesus taught about the Lord's Supper on the night
of Passover. Just as Passover celebrated
deliverance from slavery in Egypt, so the Lord's
Supper celebrates deliverance from sin by Christ's
death. I believe in my heart that participating in
the Lord's Supper is essential to Christian faith
and strengthens us spiritually. I am in my home*

church on first Sunday's, because I feel with all my heart that the Lord's Supper is for me; and I knew Coco would understand this scripture in like manner, and act on it. Coco began to come to church.

I have learned more about how I should live by going to church, and hearing the word of God. And, it's a joy to congregate with people who love the Lord. I began to learn the praise and worship songs, and I began to apply the scriptures via the preached sermons to my life. God was working on me and shaping my life, spiritually, and I wanted Coco to get on the band wagon for her blessings, too. Coco rededicated her life to Christ, she began to attend church on a regular basis; and she began to live for God. God blessed, and Coco received her business degree in 1998, praise God!

Coco also began to travel with her best friend, to visit Corie Blount in Los Angeles, a

brother who played for the Lakers. As their
relationship grew, Coco confided in me regarding
their friendship. And the trials, tribulations and
the negative and positive feedback she received
from dating a professional basketball player. In
the midst of her happiness, the Holy Spirit
continued to use me to witness to Coco.

I praise God, Coco rededicated her life to
God, when she was 26 years old. As I look back
over this time in my and Coco's life, it was the
word of God, His conviction and His will to bring
Coco back to Him. Coco's life took off, in a fast
lane she reveled in, and who can blame her?

Coco was falling in love with a decent man,
who loved and respected her, and who also made
millions of dollars a year, playing professional
basketball. She was very happy. Coco and I
continued to communicate. We would sit for hours
talking about her relationship, as Coco talked and

I listened. Within the many conversations, Coco would inquire about my abstinence. Again, I was dating, but still a single sister and I did not want to push my promise to God onto her life. I wanted Coco to be happy, and I wanted her to enjoy her life to the fullest. Enjoying life to the fullest and sharing my life with a man is one of my heart's desires, and at that time, this was one of Coco's desires, too.

Coco was receiving this blessing, and I was happy. But with an expectant heart, I was still holding my hand out to God, like a child does to her Father when he is passing out quarters, to his daughters. I often wondered when God was going to "dish" this kind of blessing my way.

As Coco discussed her blessings and her happiness, she failed to realize that I was a sister too, who wanted a blessing from God. Coco never once asked me about my male friends, or whom I was dating at the time. If I had asked Coco the name of the guy I had been dating, she would have been clueless. I began to look at our relationship from the outside. We were little girls again, and Coco was confiding in me, as if all her happiness or problems were the only thing that mattered in life.

My little sister never once wanted to know about me and my happiness or my problems in life. While hanging around Coco, I would have feelings of happiness for her, because, I could see and feel this sister's glee. We both knew that her gladness was founded on the blessings of God. This fact alone is what kept me during this time in my and Coco's friendship.

Side Bar:

My sisters, if I can offer a small amount of advice. When God is blessing you, please show a little humility during your season. Your family and friends will share your joy, but they have feelings too. And, if life is not going as well for them, please have a little empathy for their feelings.

Bless Coco's heart, she needed someone to listen to her, regarding her relationship with Corie, and God blessed me to be right by her side. I would have had it no other way. I was very happy for Coco; I knew her past, and what she experienced in her previous relationships. Coco and Corie's relationship began to grow and they were discussing marriage.

Coco also wanted to know more and more about my promise to God on abstaining. Honestly, I did not want to witness to Coco in the fornication department, but the Holy Spirit continued to lead me to do so, regarding sexual morality. Coco was blatantly sinning against God and I did not want to intrude on her life with my witnessing.

52

I may have had an agenda, but God's plan will always prevail. God was blessing Coco. This sister's season was at hand, and she was fully reaping the harvest, but conviction was flourishing in her heart, too. As God began to convict Coco's heart, the realization began to materialize within her, that having sex outside of marriage was wrong. Based on the word of God, but she wanted and needed to be told. She wanted me to tell her.

I love Coco, and I enjoyed seeing her happy. I saw her tears after her relationship with her ex-boyfriend. I was now seeing her on this other side, a more positive side, of her life, having a decent man, was so accepting and peaceful for Coco. Her happiness made me happy for her and her life. Because I enjoyed seeing her happiness, I did not want to get involved. I did not want to "force" my walk of abstinence on anyone. I felt that my plight and the promise in my life was between God and me.

When there is an anointing on your life, God's covering is so strong that the people who are in your life will be affected by the blanket. My cup was overflowing, and Coco began to taste the sweetness of God's anointing, too. God began to convict my heart, because of my silence; and my lack of witnessing to Coco. The Holy Spirit moved my heart to confront Coco. After I prayed and fasted, I explained to Coco via scripture. Please remember Coco is blessed with an obedient heart, and she will adhere to God's word.

1 Corinthians chapter 6, verses 18 – 20

16 "Flee fornication. Every sin that a man doeth is without the body; but he that committeth fornication sinneth against his own body. (19) What? Know ye not that your body is the temple of the Holy Ghost which is in you, which ye have to God, and ye are not your own?"

1 Corinthians chapter 6, *(continued)* **verse 20,**
"For ye are bought with a price: therefore glorify God in your body, and in your spirit, which are God's."

Sex outside of marriage hurts God. It shows that we are following our own desires, instead of the leading of the Holy Spirit and God's law. I knew in my heart that once Coco read these scriptures, she would make the same promise to God that I did, when I was 27.

God blessed, Coco was not angry with me, nor did she tell me to mind my business, she asked that we, pray, touch, agree and fast for her sake.

Matthew chapter 18, verse 19

"Again I say unto you, That if two of you shall agree on earth as touching anything that they shall ask, it shall be done for them of my Father which is in heaven."

Whenever I prayed and fasted with friends, we would always hold hands, and recite this scripture. We held hands, believing God through His word, claiming victory.

Alone, Coco went into prayer and another fast, seeking a confirmation from God regarding Corie. She wanted to know if Corie was the man God chose for her life and her future. Coco wanted God to control every aspect, decision and plan in her life. She was seeking God's will, first. Within a week of our conversation and fasting, Coco confronted Corie, and explained to him that what they had been doing was against God.

Needless to say, Corie was not happy. He asked her why she had made the decision so far into their relationship. Corie asked "You were not acting like this in the beginning of the relationship, why all this now? I told you that we were going to get married, but I am not ready yet."

Coco (God bless her heart) replied... "If you think I am going to wait years on you to make up your mind, we can split now. I have sinned against my God repeatedly, and it must stop now. I will not make love to you again, until we are married."

My sisters, Coco became Mrs. Corie Blount four months later, in a private ceremony. It was all a secret, but I knew. God is good. God continued to bless Coco and Corie, about five months after their wedding Coco was pregnant, and six months later Coco and Corie were married in a more traditional ceremony, at The Oakley Full Gospel Baptist Church. Needless to say, I was one of the seven bridesmaids.

And I must state, Coco and Corie's wedding was one of the most beautiful and extravagant weddings I have ever had the pleasure to witness. It was a beautiful day for a beautiful pair. Three months following, on September 7, 2000, Corie Blount, Jr. (C.J.) was born. God is good, smile.

Chapter 4

My Sister-Girlfriend, Dionne

Proverbs chapter 18, verse 24

"A man that hath friends, must show himself friendly: and there is a friend that sticketh closer than a brother."

I love my sister-girlfriend Dionne. Dionne and I have been friends for more than 15 years, and, I feel as if we are twin sisters. Dionne and I share so many like qualities: If Dionne gave a party and you were invited, she would make sure that you feel as though you were the reason the party was given, and so would I. If Dionne had two dollars in her pocket, and you needed one, she would give you both dollars, just in case you came up short. So would I.

Dionne is so giving and loving, and she loves to hug and kiss her people too. Dionne is the type of person who will make you feel better if you are having a bad day. It's like she was born with an innate ability to sooth a negative situation, and simply make a person feel better. Everyone loves to hang out with Dionne; she is the definition of fun and having a good time.

Dionne and I met on the job, where we worked together for more than three years. Dionne and her family lived on the HillTop too. I knew of her, but we were never really good friends, until we worked together. Dionne is an Army brat via her father, who was a very strict man. Dionne has two sisters, one older and one younger, Dionne states that she, too, suffers from the middle child syndrome.

Dionne was "saved" at the age of 12, and like most of us, she had fallen into some hard times and she backslid. Dionne had her first son, Tony, at the age of 16, and her parents put her out of the house. Her Mother's best friend, "Mommy Sharon," took her in, and continued to raise Dionne and her new baby.

Needless to say, this event in Dionne's life was very hurtful and traumatic. Dionne's family and the baby's father's family thought Dionne was lying due to the fact that she had the dates of conception mixed up. Dionne was sixteen, a senior in high school, thrown out of her house, and the father of the baby she was carrying denied the child. God blessed Dionne, and she was able to press her way forward, and make a good life for her and her child. Dionne is a very strong, positive person, and a survivor, she is fully aware that God has blessed her and her life.

For years, Dionne and I have spent one or two Saturdays a month together, going to dinner, movies, concerts and plays. I can honestly say that Dionne was my "date" on several occasions. While Dionne loved to hang out at the clubs, I was not the type of person to frequent night clubs or bars. So, after Dionne and I went to the movies on a Saturday night, I would usually drop her off at the club, where she would hook up with her other girlfriends. I would go hang out with the guy I was

dating at the time. We were in our early to mid
twenties.

One factor Dionne and I had in common
was how much we loved to talk and that in our
20's we were very immature, and very spoiled.
Dionne and I fell out all the time, over very minor
issues. We would be talking one week, and mad at
each other the following week. And this went on
for years. Once when we had fallen out, we did
not speak for several weeks. But when we did
"make-up" we were so happy, and still somewhat
mad at each other, for the stubborn attitude, that
kept our friendship apart.

After that, we made a pact with one another
that we were not going to let the sun go down over
an issue. If we made one another mad, we had to
discuss the issue before the night ended. This
promise we made one another truly blessed us. As
sister-girlfriends, we may not agree with one

another on every issue, but we learned to respect each other's opinion, and to move on.

My sisters, do you have a friend who is a magnet for "sorry" men? I do, and it's Dionne. Dionne was more into quantity than quality; any man who would ask Dionne for her number got it. Dionne dated all types of men, from strippers to Asian men. I believe Dionne was looking for the love she missed during her childhood.

At the age of 22 Dionne had her second baby, Alexis, my god-daughter. At the time Dionne lived with Alexis' daddy. We continued to hang out together. At the age of 30 Dionne had another baby, Shayla, and she lived with Shayla's daddy too. Bless Dionne's heart, every man she lived with, she also physically fought, and I was there to back her up without any questions.

When I rededicated my life to God, I began to witness to Dionne, too. She was my closest *friend at the time, and I wanted her to know what was happening in my life. One of the many reasons why I love Dionne is because she is a friend that I can tell anything and everything and she will not judge me, nor will her love for me and our friendship fade away. Dionne will talk about what is happening in her life and we will discuss the situation. When she is done, she will open the door for me to talk about my life, my happiness, and what is going on in my walk with God.*

We would sit for hours at the park, on the street curb, on her porch, in her house, out eating dinner, and talk about my plight in life. And, to consider the fact that Dionne does not attend church on a regular basis, she always gave me an encouraging word. Dionne would say, "Lisa, what you are doing is a good thing, and you can have a baby if you really want to, right now. You really do not have to wait on God. But, you really want to wait on God, and you can never go wrong with a dream like this. Hold on Lisa, because when your time comes, (pregnancy) we are going to spoil you rotten."

I love Dionne. She could have several issues to deal with and three kids to take care of, but she always had the time to hang out with me. I could go to Dionne's house at anytime of the day, without calling, and we would just hang out, watch movies, play with her kids, eat and talk all night long. But, when we went out, Dionne would also insist on paying for the movies, or dinner and she did not work. God blessed Dionne with such a nurturing and giving heart, thank you Jesus! As I look back over my plight, I can see how God made my life a little easier with friends like Dionne.

After the age of 30, I had made a declaration of no more dating"unsaved" men. I must admit to you, that announcement did not last long. All of my friends had men, and some were married, and I wanted a man, too. I had very few dates with "saved" men, and I was lonely for male company and attention. Also, some of my girlfriends were going to parties with their men, and only inviting their friends who had men.

Dionne was the only friend who would invite me to hang out with her and her man. If one of Dionne's guys was having a party to watch the fight on HBO or Pay-Per-View, Dionne invited me. If one of her guys was having a Super Bowl party, I was asked to come and join in on the fun. Dionne knew in her heart that I was never a threat. I would never try to talk to one of my girlfriend's man. That act goes against everything that is within me, and in my life.

I would include Dionne on some of my dates, too. My sisters, I am sure some of you know what its like to sit home on Saturday nights alone, while your friends are out with their men. It's not a good feeling. On one occasion, I was dating a firefighter, who was a minister, divorced, and on the verge of backsliding. He took me to a sports bar, to watch a game of football (I love all sports, and I am currently trying my hand at golf (I am terrible at the game, but given time, I will become a better player.)) I invited Dionne, and we had the best time. He looked after me and Dionne, and the three of us bonded. He understood fully why I invited Dionne to come along.

Dionne was never a fifth wheel, because we, my date and I, made sure she felt comfortable. She never once felt left out. I smile, because I remember, when I was the third person, Dionne also made me feel comfortable. I thank God for blessing Dionne's heart in understanding my plight, and including me in her life. Although

Dionne always kept a man, our friendship never diminished, praise God.

In our 30's, Dionne was no longer living with a man, praise God. The Holy Spirit began to work on my witnessing to Dionne about abstinence. Every time we hung out, I would talk about how sleeping with men outside of marriage is a blatant sin against God. Dionne would never comment on her life, but she continued to uplift me and my life, on waiting for God. Over one dinner, Dionne proudly announced, "Lisa, I have not had sex for three months." You all know that I was grinning hard.

I ordered a birthday cake to celebrate the good news. And from that point on, Dionne gave me updates on her abstinence. My sister-girl friend has been abstaining for over two years. The Holy Spirit was working on Dionne, too, through

*my witnessing. God is good. Dionne is now
talking about marriage, and waiting on God.*

Proverbs chapter 18, verse 24

*"A man that hath friends, must show himself
friendly: and there is a friend that sticketh closer
than a brother."*

*I love this verse, even though it's somewhat hard
to understand. But after researching this scripture
and praying for understanding, this is what I got:
A man that has many friends may come to ruin; but
if you have just one good friend, he will stick
closer to you than a brother or a sister. It all goes
back to quantity versus quality.*

*It's better to have one good friend that will
stick with you through the good times and the bad,
than to have several superficial friends and
acquaintances. And, I can honestly say, that
Dionne is the one person/friend that has been by*

my side through my plight. Dionne was in my life before my promise to God and she has remained by my side during this plight. I know with all my heart, Dionne will be there to help me praise God for the victory! I love you, Dionne!

Chapter 5

My Spiritual Sister, Diana

Job chapter 36, verse 16

"He is wooing you from the jaws of distress to a spacious place free from restriction, to the comfort of your table laden with choice food."

(The NIV (New International Version) Study Bible)

Diana and I have been friends for more than 15 years, Diana and I worked together for a very short period of time, but our friendship was sealed on the very same day we met. Diana has been "saved" for more than 22 years, since the age of 11. She attends New Life Apostolic Church, in Columbus, Ohio. Diana has a twin sister, Diane. And, she works for the same company too. I can remember how outspoken and carefree the twins were. They would sing gospel songs, walking down the hall, at work.

They would praise God in the break room and they were so friendly, to everyone. One could see that they loved the Lord, and His anointing was upon their lives. Needless to say, some people had bad things to say about the twins, but I was intrigued. I loved their boldness, at this time in my life, I had backslidden from church, and I believe God was working on me through the twins.

Diana would witness to me and everyone in our department on a daily basis and I loved her positive personality. By the grace of God, we became fast friends.

Diana married a man of God, Jeff, on July 17, 1991, in a very private and beautiful ceremony. One year after their marriage, God blessed the couple to buy their first house. Two years after the house, on March 21, 1994, Diana gave birth to their son, Terrell. Six years later, on April 2, 2002 baby Olivia was born. I was at the hospital the same day, and everyday following until Diana was released. Diana and Jeff had waited a long time on Olivia to bless their lives. I can remember when Diana was trying to get pregnant; I would send her information on ovulation. I once took a print-out to her home, but she was out shopping. Her husband took the information, and after reading it over in detail, the brother grinned so hard.

Diana was pregnant within weeks. Diana is a wonderful, caring and loving mother I only hope and pray that God will bless me to have the same characteristics when He blesses me with a family.

Diana and her twin sister are almost inseparable. They are big time shoppers, the best of friends, and they have been on their own, helping one another grow into adulthood since the age of 18. God has truly blessed the twins. The devil tried in so many ways to destroy Diana and Diane. At the age of 4, their parents divorced, leaving the twins emotionally distraught.

Diana was hit by a drunk driver the same year. And, when the twins were at the age of 10, both sisters contemplated suicide. Diana and Diane had devised private and separate ways to take their own lives. God blessed, and months later the twins gave their lives to Jesus Christ on their 11th birthday.

Shortly afterward, Diana was hit by another car, I praise God for keeping Diana and her twin, because both sisters have truly been a blessing to my life, their families and their church families. Diana is one of my greatest blessings from God; from the first day of that introduction, Diana has been encouraging me on the word of God. Although Diana had a family, worked full time, and is the Superintendent of her church's Sunday school, Diana always found time to hang out with me. We would go shopping or to dinner, and then more shopping, smile.

Diana and I hung out once a month, and during those times, Diana would inform me of what was happening in her church, personal and work life. And like Dionne, she always asked how I was doing, if I needed anything, and she would give me encouraging scriptures. I would receive calls on my voice mail, where Diana would insist *that I read a certain scripture. She would say, "Lisa, God has placed you so heavy on my heart. I want you to read, and meditate on **Hebrews chapter 10, verses 35 – 38.** I promise you will be blessed Lisa. I love you, and we must get together soon, to shop."*

Side Bar:

I am very thankful for Diana, she could have been pointing her finger at me, like the friends of Job or she could have asked me what type of sin I committed. She could have insisted that I pray more, fast more, or seek God more. Instead, she gave me scripture. My sisters, you will know if you have a true friend of God, if she sticks by your side during your trials and tribulations, and displays a positive and optimistic outlook on life, encouraging with the word of God, and providing unconditional love.

I remember one trial that tested our friendship, Diana's baby girl Olivia was to be christened on May 5, 2002, and I was expected to attend the ceremony. That early morning God had placed a lady on my heart so strongly, and He wanted me to lay hands on her and pray for her condition. I thought my first priority was Olivia and witnessing her christening, but, God had other plans.

I prayed, "Father, this lady does not attend Oakley. How will I know she will even be there, and it's not like me to say that I will do something or be in a particular place and not show up." No answer from God. I went to Oakley, and the lady was in the pew right behind me. I knew what I had to do, what I must do, obey God. I was somewhat worried about how Diana would respond. Her baby girl, her long awaited blessing from God, was having her very first formal ceremony, and I was not going to be in attendance.

After church, I immediately called Diana to explain. She listened, and although I was very nervous, I informed Diana about my morning. Diana replied, "Lisa, I knew it had to be something that God was doing in you. It was a beautiful christening and I took pictures for you, now when are we getting together to shop?" I could only praise God.

And I prayed that God would bless me with a spirit of understanding, so that if this kind of thing ever happened to me, I would have the patience and the maturity to listen first, and realize that everything does not revolve around Lisa, and react as God would have me.

I can remember another instance when Diana had my back, spiritually, I had gone

through something with another friend of mine,
and the issue weighed heavily on my heart.
And, on top of everything else, my birthday was
approaching, and, I had no one to spend my day
with. Diana took a vacation day and we had lunch
and shopped all day. I confided in Diana about
how my wait on God has truly saddened me, and
made me question so many things in life, and how
God has broken my heart through this tribulation
and test.

Diana replied, "Lisa, unfortunately we do
not know how long our Father is going to make
you wait, but I do know that He will bless you for
your faithfulness. Lisa, you have not stopped
tithing. You continue to pray and fast, and if
anyone needs help you are the first to arrive. Lisa,
I believe in my heart what the word of God says in
Galatians chapter 6, verse 7, *'Be not deceived;*
God is not mocked: for whatsoever a man soweth,

that shall he also reap.' Lisa, God has blessed you with a good and kind heart, you will give a bum on the street your last dollar. He will bless you, just hold on. You will reap what you have sown." I praise God for blessing me with a friend like Diana.

Because I just work part-time, Diana would sometimes pay for my dinner during our shopping sprees. Diana and I would also attend plays and movies together. On one occasion, Diana had organized a group to attend a play that was coming to Columbus.

Diana stated that she was going to buy my ticket. And, that she simply wanted me to come along with her and her First Lady, Sister Scott and Sister Smith from her church. The play was really funny, and we were having a really good time. During the play, Diana leaned close to her First Lady, and made the silliest face, simply playing

and kidding around as girlfriends will do. Sister
Scott missed the "face" but I caught it, and Diana
and I laughed at least 20 minutes about her
silliness.

I am grinning now, about the laughter we
shared. I laughed so hard that I cried, and
everyone around us wanted to know what we were
laughing at. We could not calm down to explain
that it was so minor and silly, and that it could not
be put in plain words at that time. But we enjoyed
the night, and the issues we had in life were set
aside. Our trials and tribulations were second and
third hand that night. Sisterhood and being with
good people, people who love you, prevailed.
Laughter is good for the heart, and spirit, too.

Job chapter 36, verse 16

*"He is wooing you from the jaws of distress to a
spacious place free from restriction, to the comfort
of your table laden with choice food."*

The Holy Spirit gave me this scripture for Diana's chapter; I believe that I had exhausted most of the scriptures on friends and friendship. I praise God this scripture is so fitting for this chapter on my spiritual sister, Diana. This scripture is from the friend of Job, Elihu.

It's Elihu's third speech to Job and it's one of the most encouraging statements from the so-called friends of Job. Elihu encourages Job, as God has blessed Diana to encourage me. Elihu states that God is wooing you. He is loving and courting you through your trials, out of the jaws of future distress (pain). And, this act (of wooing) will advance you toward a place in your life that will be free of all restrictions and inhibitions.

*And, once you overcome your trials and tribulations, (with the help of the Holy Spirit) your table (life) will be laden (full) with choice food (blessings). Praise God, **Job chapter 36, verse 16,*** *summarizes Diana's mission to provide positive encouragement within my life. I am blessed to have Diana in my life, a real friend, grounded in God, to be right by my side, during my walk through the wilderness.*

Chapter 6

My Best Friend, Monica

Proverbs chapter 13, verse 20

"He that walketh with wise men shall be wise: but a companion of fools shall be destroyed."

I love my best friend Monica, dearly. At the age of 35, I thank God for blessing me with a best friend, who is saved, filled with the Holy Spirit, and most of all, a sister who fears God. Monica and I have only been friends for three short years, and looking over my circle of friends, I would have never thought God would have blessed me to have Monica as my best friend. Monica and I began our informal friendship at a candle party she invited me to at her home. I knew Monica was a cool sister when she reached up and ate right from my plate and never broke stride with the current conversation. And she was reshaping my eyebrows too, all at her candle party. From that day on, God began to evolve our relationship.

Monica had backslidden from church and God began to convict my heart heavily to witness to Monica. Monica knew God's word and the will of God, but like most of us, Monica allowed her issues in life to overpower her good judgment regarding the church. The last thing I wanted to do was to tell this sister that she needed to rededicate her life to Christ. I did not want to portray a self-righteous, finger-pointing, haughty sister. But, I was learning more and more about obedience to God, and His conviction. And obedience is better than sacrifice. I would have sacrificed my newfound friendship with Monica to obey God.

Praise God, Monica rededicated her life to Christ, and God immediately blessed Monica with a ministry, The Oakley Full Gospel Baptist Church's Liturgical Dance Ministry. God has truly blessed Monica. She graduated Cum Laude from Bennett College with a Bachelors degree in Biology, and a minor in Chemistry. She is a member of Alpha Kappa Alpha Sorority, Inc. Monica also belongs to the Order of Eastern Star, a member of Daughter of Isis, and she is a member of the 100 Women Coalition, Columbus Chapter; and she is the President of the African Jewels Book Club.

Like many girlfriends, Monica and I had our share of "fall-outs," and the friendship was forced through the wringer, the dryer and more. Monica had the mindset that once she had a major disagreement with a friend, she was completely through with the entire relationship. She had no problem writing people off and out of her life. During this time, God had delivered me from holding grudges.

So when Monica and I had disagreements, she immediately ended our friendship, while I was trying my best not to hold a grudge. But, I did not depend totally on God to help me after my deliverance. So I still held grudges, and our *friendship suffered. Monica had the tendency to compare and compete with her friends.*

I attributed her disposition to the kind of childhood she experienced. Monica was a loner, she was overweight, and the kids in her neighborhood reminded her of it daily. On the other hand, I was (most times) the leader of the basketball team, and one of many who won the neighborhood kickball game by kicking the ball the farthest. The kids I grew up with were too busy trying to improve their athletic skills and enjoying life as a kid, to ridicule and tease all the time. We shared everything. If my birthday present was a new bike, you had better believe Coco and her brother Tyrone would be riding that same bike by the end of the day.

When Monica and I were at the age of 32, Monica began dating a brother with whom she shared a close friendship, for more than 10 years.

And, like most women, Monica had experienced her share of "bad" relationships with men. God began to "open" Monica's eyes regarding this brother, and she began to realize that no other man had treated her the way this man had. God showed Monica this man was truly a blessing to her and her life.

Monica began to pray and fast, seeking God's confirmation regarding this man and their future together. Once God confirmed Monica's prayers, the two made personal commitments to one another. There were countless times I had to have a listening ear while Monica discussed her relationship with her man, their outings, movies, concerts, and their different dates and gatherings as couples, with her other girlfriends and their men. At times I felt left out, but at this time we were at the age of 33 and 34, and I was not sure about Monica and our friendship.

I was unable to define the relationship. I categorized her as an associate, and I simply listened to her blessings. I thank God for blessing me with an open heart to listen and receive news regarding my friends. During the many conversations, my thoughts took me to my past and the fun I had with the men I dated, and to my future and the excitement I would experience with the man God has for me. And I was still dating and I was so very close to Dionne, so my life was not completely empty.

Monica had one dilemma within her relationship with her man: He had not rededicated his life to Christ. Through prayer and fasting, Monica knew God had blessed her with this man, and he was the love of her life. But there would never be a marriage without his rededication to Christ. Monica went through the process of

88

begging her man to come to church, praying, fasting and more pleading.

In the midst of Monica's predicament with her man, God began to convict her heart because she was having sex with the man she loved. And, she began to confide in me regarding this heaviness on her heart. As I look back over the many conversations, I see the Holy Spirit's work within the long discussions, regarding my promise to God and abstinence. The Holy Spirit is so awesome: He blesses you and the people within your life when you are not even aware of what is happening.

I had no intention of opening my big mouth to Monica, regarding the sin of having sex outside of marriage, because she was fully aware of her own sin. But, my promise to God and my lifestyle became prevalent within our friendship and our many conversations.

I believe in my heart, God will convict you through another Christian. If God has blessed you with a humble heart, and you are open to receive a positive message or witness, God will use a family member or a close friend to bring His conviction. I praise God I never once said anything against Monica and her relationship with her man. I was learning how to simply be quiet, and God blessed me with a listening ear.

Again, I did not want to come off as a self-righteous sister. My abstinence was the least I could do for God, and the promise I made God was between Him and I. And, I was the last person who needed to be put on a pedestal for abstaining from sex. I never hesitated to inform all my friends that it's my reasonable service to God. And, I praise God for blessing me with the help of the Holy Spirit.

Romans chapter 12, verse 1

*"I beseech you therefore, brethren, by the mercies
of God, that ye present your bodies a living
sacrifice, holy, acceptable unto God, which is your
reasonable service."*

*I believe that God wants us to offer ourselves as
living sacrifices to His word, His commandments,
and His will for our lives. Abstaining from sexual
intercourse is my reasonable service. It's the least
I can do for God. And, I never bragged about this
area of my life, and to be honest, there was nothing
to brag about. In this area of my life, I was
without sin and in no way was I to be placed on a
pedestal. So, I allowed no one to make more of my
situation than it really was, obeying the word of
God.*

*Monica continued to pray and fast for her
relationship with her man. Monica is a wonderful
communicator. She has several prayer and fasting*

partners. She would also seek an elder in the church and some of her close girlfriends for the mission, and God blessed.

Monica knew the sin she was committing was wrong, but the love and closeness she shared with this man was something tangible within her life she did not want to lose or give up. God continued to bless the couple. And, when Monica acted on her heart's conviction regarding sex outside of marriage, she denied her man of further sexual activity until marriage.

Monica and her man no longer stayed every night with each other. And if they happened to stay with one another, they slept in different bedrooms. During their many vacations together they ordered double beds, and limited their vacation trips to weekends. They began to pray and fast together; their love was flourishing without the stain of the sin: sex outside of marriage.

1 Corinthians chapter 7, verse 14

"For the unbelieving husband is sanctified by the wife, and the unbelieving wife is sanctified by the husband: else were your children unclean; but now are they holy."

Although Monica and her man were not married, God blessed, due to Monica's diligent prayer life, her fasting and trusting in God to bring her man back to Him. Their relationship grew, in the name of Jesus Christ. God had blessed Monica with such an awesome anointing, and her man received the extra blessings that spilled from Monica's plate. Monica's man believed in God and he was sanctified (covered) by his woman. God is good.

Monica no longer had to ask her love to come to church. The brother came on his own accord. Considering this brother is a firefighter, he would leave work at 8am, and make it to the 10:45am church service. I believe God began to convict his heart, too. I like this brother because he has always supported Monica in every avenue of life, regarding her spiritual walk, respecting her fasting, her prayer life, her church ministry, and all other avenues regarding the betterment of her life.

At the age of 35 and in the month of September 2001, Monica and I went on a two-week fast together. In our prayer we asked God to bless our friendship and we also asked God to bless us with one personal and separate desire of our hearts. Monica and I held hands, and recited, **Matthew chapter 18, verse 19,** *"Again I say unto you, That if two of you shall agree on earth as touching anything that they shall ask, it shall be done for them of my Father which is in heaven."*

Monica is from Detroit, Michigan, and very much a "Mama's girl" and she desperately wanted to move back home. Although she had established a life in Columbus, Ohio, she was deeply missing her family. Monica's personal desire, within the fast, was for God to confirm her life in Columbus or open a door to move back home. My personal desire within the fast was for God to have mercy on me, and bless me with at least one of my heart's desires.

The blessing of our individual desires: God blessed Monica with a dream. She was in our church, The Oakley Full Gospel Baptist Church, marrying her man. Her mother was there, and I was standing right beside her; and her family and friends were present. Needless to say, Monica was ecstatic, and the clamor of her thoughts and feelings regarding moving back home to Detroit became silent.

This sister was fully aware that she was in God's perfect will regarding her life. My individual blessing: God blessed me with the vision to write this book. He outlined the book, gave me scriptures, and a vision of the front cover. He informed me that I must go on a fast every time I wrote, (allowing the Holy Spirit to lead). God made the vision so clear, I began writing, with the help of the Holy Spirit the following week.

Matthew chapter 6, verses 16 – 18

(16). "Moreover when ye fast, be not, as the hypocrites, of a sad countenance: for they disfigure their faces, that they may appear unto men to fast. Verily I say unto you, Thy have their reward. (17). But thou, when thou fastest, anoint thine head, and wash thy fast; (18). That thou appear not unto men to fast, but unto thy Father, which seeth in secret, shall reward thee openly."

Fasting is going without food to clear your mind and heart to better receive instruction from God.

96

This is the primary reason why I fast. At times when I am tripping, complaining, or whining about my plight, the Holy Spirit moves within my heart to fast. It clears the muddy waters of my life, helping me to get past what I think that I am lacking, and what I do not have in my life. Fasting helps me channel in on God and His will for my life. Some people say that you shouldn't go on a fast unless God instructs you to do so. Let us not put God in a box. If you are tripping, complaining etc. etc. about your life, and if you want to effectively hear the voice of God, I urge you to turn over your plate. Once you turn over that plate, your blessings begin. God will bless your willingness and your desire to move closer to Him. God is good.

Monica's man asked her to marry him in the middle of November 2001. God had blessed Monica with her heart's desire and her man rededicated his life to Jesus Christ the following week. God is good. The wedding date was set for December 8, 2001 and Monica informed everyone the wedding was going to be a private affair, only family and close friends. Monica informed me, "I want you to come to my wedding and just be pretty. There should be some single men there." Needless to say, I was surprised, and hurt. I thought that I was going to be standing next to Monica, or somewhere close within her lineup.

My feelings were hurt. I thought that once you were blessed to have a wedding, all of your close girlfriends just had to be in your line up, Monica proved me wrong. I was very upset, and I began to pray and fast, asking God for some type of guidance. How could I remain close friends with this sister? I began to think, "Where is this sister's loyalty?" After Monica's engagement, our line of communication was cut in half. We managed to talk, but very little.

On one occasion Monica was a little stressed. Her Sorority sisters were dragging their feet about setting up her bridal shower. I stepped in and informed Monica that I would handle it, and that I would make sure I included everyone, so that we all could give her the shower and no one would feel left out.

I called Monica's friends in Columbus, Detroit, Baltimore, and one in New York. I set the time, date, and the restaurant. I purchased the cake, balloons, decorations, paid for Monica's dinner and more. I figured this sister deserved better. I was a witness to the countless times Monica was there for her friends, and how she backed these sisters on many occasions and functions.

At the bridal party, most of the sisters were unfriendly and rude to me, and Monica lead the pack. I was fully aware that Monica had informed everyone that I ended our friendship because I was not a part of her wedding. I can remember during the shower, I looked across the table at Monica to simply give her a small smile, a wink, to simply let her know that everything would be all right, and that this issue between us would pass (I still had some hope left.) As I looked down the table at Monica, at that same moment, Monica accused me of cheating at one of the bridal shower games (and to be honest, I like to cheat at games, but Monica was wrong this time).

At the closing of the shower, Monica stood and gave a small speech, and she handed out presents to her mother-in-law-to-be, a present to one of her sorority sisters, and presents to two more sisters, thanking them for giving her the shower. I received no present, not even a thank you. I was hurt. After the shower, I immediately called my sister-girlfriend, Dionne. I asked Dionne, "If I was to be married, and I failed to have you in my lineup, would you still be my friend?" Dionne replied, "Hell no, Lisa. Stop tripping." I love my Dionne. I had to see if I was wrong. I wanted to know what happened, and how did this whole issue become so bad so quickly?

The next day in church, as I sat beside my "pew-partner" Vicki, who is the head of Oakley's New Member's Ministry. I informed her of what happened, but, I left out the minor details I stated that it was a regular party, not a bridal shower because I did not want Vicki in this mess with me and Monica. I could not understand how a child of God could act in such a way. Vicki summed up this terrible trial when she replied, "Lisa, when a person steps out of the will of God, the devil steps

in and causes havoc in their life and the people
they are close to.

Do not fret. The Bible says in **2
Thessalonians chapter 3, verse 13,** *be not weary
in your well doing, God will bless you." I thanked
God for Vicki that day, and I continued to pray
and ask God to keep me from wallowing in my
anger towards Monica. Monica and her man were
married on December 10, 2001.*

*God laid on my heart that I had to forgive
Monica and I did. I informed Monica that I
forgave her for all that had happened. Monica
called me and asked if we could have lunch to talk
about this issue. I informed Monica that I did not
want to debate with her. I felt any excuse she gave
would make matters worse. We had lunch and
talked, and bless Monica's heart, the sister prayed
and fasted before we met for lunch, and she*

apologized for all that had happened, and all was well.

I called Monica a few weeks later to simply say hi, because I had not heard from her. Monica stated that she was too busy, and that her husband had to make her go to bed the night before to get some rest. Needless to say, I vowed that I would not call Monica again.

Side Bar*:*

I once had an associate, Jacquie explain to me that after marriage, she no longer had time for her friends and that her husband was her friend now. I was quiet during this conversation. Immediately afterwards, I prayed and asked God to help me to manage my time, so that I would not ever tell a friend that I was to busy to hang out, or to talk on the phone, or to go shopping.

I would never expect my future husband to be everything in my life, and I would never want him to cover all my needs as a daughter, sister and friend. Recently Ching-Yi called me, and left a message. She stated that she knew that I was very busy, but if I could go shopping with her, she really wanted to hang out with me. I immediately called Ching-Yi back, and explained that I will never be too busy to bond with her, never.

When God blesses me with my husband, this man of God will not only bless my life, but he will be a blessing to my family and friends' lives, too. Monica and I did not talk for several weeks, and Monica stated in church, that I was jealous of her. The devil knows how to work his magic. I was so angry Monica was definitely outside my friendship boundaries. Any friend or former friend of mine would never use the word jealous in the same sentence with me.

Monica called me and wanted to talk again, stating that she believed that it was God's will that *she and I be friends. 'The anointing that God blessed us with is so strong, how could we not be friends, Lisa?" she said. I informed Monica that I was not going to meet with her again, and that I learned several lessons from this mess. The most important lesson I learned is that when God blesses me I must not act a fool in my blessing.*

God informed me that I must forgive Monica once more, but I did not have to be in the midst of Monica's life, ever again. I forgave Monica. For the life of me, I simply do not understand why I had to go through this trial, when I had so much on my plate. I cannot figure out why at the age of 35, I declared someone my best friend, and that so called best friend treated me like dirt, for no reason. You see, my hopes were too high.

I believed in having a best friend, the sisterhood of friends, and all the positive effects a good and sound friendship can provide. Monica's friendship blew that theory.

Chapter 7

In My 10th Year of Waiting...

Job chapter 10, verse 18

"Why then did you bring me out of the womb? I wish I had died before any eye saw me."

(The NIV (New International Version) Study Bible)

*Through the mist of my pain and the
heartache of my life, I speak freely to you Father,
because I have nothing to lose. You my Father
have broken my heart, and through my tears, I will
hold not one thought back. Please condemn me no
longer with the guilty plea that is before me.*

*Please my Father, show me what I have
done to deserve 10 years of waiting. I know your
people will state that the children of God do not
deserve anything, that we are all mere particles of
dirt. Father, why did you have me born? Father,
your plan and perfect will is good, but from my
plight, looking up to you, Father, it seems as if you
are giving me a hard time daily.*

*Father, what was it that you placed in me, in
my heart, or did you see something special in me,
to force me through such a trial? Father you
shaped my heart, soul and mind, into what you will
have me, will you ever bless me, with the desires of*

my heart? Will you ever mend my heart? Will the puzzle of my life ever fit together? The "wicked" are more blessed than I am, Father, I have tithed for over 12 years, and my debt is still greater than $30,000. I still have hope that you will crack the window in heaven and pour out a blessing just for me. Father, you blessed me with a loving heart, yet you have denied me the love of a man so that I may have a child.

But I must thank you father. You have abundantly blessed me with a loving, caring, understanding and beautiful mother. I thank you very much, Sir. And you have blessed me with three wonderful friends, in whom I know what real friends are made of. I thank you, Father. And, you have blessed me with a kind and supportive family and church family. I thank you God, for their love. I deeply feel as if my life thus far has been lived in vain, for nothing. Why was I born?

I know your eyes are greater than mine. My vision is limited, and compared to your sight, I am blind. But must you make me feel like I am unable to breathe, like I am constantly in the throws of an anxiety attack? Unlike your children, Father you are without a deadline. I know that I should not look at worldly things, but my reality is a constant. My feelings are so strong, and they run deep, because you have refined my life and heart.

Father, for more than 20 years, I have desired children. My mother gave birth to me at the age of 22 and she was able to cheer along with me at the football games. Mom shared and enjoyed her youth with her children. I am pushing toward the age of 40 and I can only hope to see my grandchildren. And Father, if another saint mentions the story of Sarah, I will scream. Must everyone be so uncaring? Please bless me to have a more caring heart and understanding spirit, so that I may take the time and patience to help someone during their trials and tribulations of life.

So Father, what is my life all about? Please enlighten me. I need understanding. I know that understanding brings forth wisdom, and wisdom is supplied through you, my Father. I need your covering. My breastplate is no more than filthy rags. It's shattered. Lord, I need your breastplate of righteousness. The breastplate will protect my heart, and your righteousness is the axle that holds my emotions and self worth together. Father, I need your protection. The emotions within my heart are like a leaf in the autumn wind, tossed to and fro.

Your conviction is strong in my life, you know that I love to sneak and eat the individually wrapped candy in the supermarkets, but, no more. Your conviction punches me in the lip, at every corner of my life. Father, my most favorite scripture: **Psalms chapter 139, verse 23 and 24,**

23 "Search me, O God, and know my heart: try

me, and know my thoughts: (24) And see if there

be any wicked way in me, and lead me in the way

everlasting." Father, you gave me that scripture

to recite, study and to love in my heart. And

Father, you still search for something. I have done

wrong. I am wrong daily. I sin daily.

You see me, and know me. You made me,

Father. So what is all this about? I am not worthy

of such a test. I guess it's to late for that

statement, because I am in the midst of this test,

hoping, praying, fasting, pleading, praying, falling

on my face before you, and seeking you, oh God,

for deliverance. Why was I born?

Father, you are fully aware that I am not a

bad woman, nor am I wicked. I will never accept

anyone calling me wicked because I know that you

have blessed my heart. No one can help me. I

tease Diana and Coco, and I have often asked my sisters "Are you praying for me? The prayers of the righteous avail much." We laugh, but Father, my heart thumps to a slower beat. It's not funny. Life is sad.

Father you made me, you molded me, you constructed my heart. You readied my disposition about facing hard times and unique people. You set up my personality to react in a positive manner although I still need help in some areas, too. Yet I feel as if I have been inside a cage on a wheel, right beside a friendly hamster. Running the wheel around and around for 10 years, going no where. Father, do you not trust me to handle more? Father it seems that I was much happier before I rededicated my life to you. I believe that you would have kept me safe, regardless, out of love.

No one ever told me about this size of heart ache, or sadness, all I want to do is to try and live

right. *All my life I have acknowledged you,
Father. I will obey you, Father. I will stay within
Your will, and I will continue to praise you,
Father, but why the secrets? Am I entitled to
anything? Dionne has a saying for my life, Father,
and I know you are fully aware of this saying. She
states, that I ask for little and receive nothing.*

*The truth hurts, but if I have done something
wrong that I have failed to repent of, please show
me, Father, so that I may ask for your forgiveness.
Unlike Job, I will never accept the feelings of
being completely doomed. Innocence, is there
such a person who is so clean? Father, I never
claimed the title. I am not doomed, and what I feel
in the bottom of my stomach is not bitterness, its
pain, from the wait and the need to be a mother.
I hurt because I was born a woman for one reason,
to reproduce.*

I would love to bring forth a child, and turn him or her over to you, like Hannah. Give me a chance, my Father. Father I am up to my ears in pain and my pillow remains wet from my tears. I have tried everything to maintain my hope in you, Father. The knot that I am hanging onto at the end of the rope is too big for my grip, I need you Father. I cry out to you.

Please stay with me. Please feel my heart. Please help me. Please bless me. It feels like you are a lion, Father, and I am a mere bunny rabbit. I have to look out for my well being at all times. I thought that you had blessed me with a best friend, but it was not so. Please Father, I ask you to bless me with more of a discerning spirit.

Please Father, please give me your hand, so that I may not go under the quick sand. I need to breathe and see the light. I need you to pull me out, and bring deliverance. I would love to rest in you and your love Father, but I am on the constant lookout. What a great day it will be when I can praise you on the other side of my plight.

Why was I born Father? I could have been a stillborn or my mother could have given me up via abortion or adoption. Why me, Father? Will my blessings outweigh this 10 year "jail" sentence? Will I ever make it over, and forget all that has happened to me? Is it time to call it quits on my life? Will you take my life before I am able to bring a life into the world, father? Please have mercy on me, please. In the name of Jesus Christ, I see myself coming out!

<u>Paraphrased from the entire 10th chapter of Job</u>

My Big Sister from God, Lisa

My big sister, my spiritual sister, my best friend;
I remember the cheer we sang back than.
C-A-T-C-H-U-P, catch-up, catch-up.
We went from cheering for Westgate Eagles,
to cheering for Christ....
HALLELUJAH, THANK YOU JESUS,
THANK YOU HOLY SPIRIT.

Ordained our friendship to be,
God has plans for you and me.
Born separately, our Father is the same,
As special as can be, no earthly man can claim.

Footsteps, sometimes I see,
That don't belong to you or me.
Jesus carries our friendship at times,
Because of my ways that still need refined.

Our friendship has taken on new life.
Your hurt is my hurt including your strife.
What God has in store we would all like to know.

The smile in your voice brings peace to my heart,
Wondering how soon for your next start.
Hopelessness in my heart I feel,
Praying that he will soon appear.

Dear Heavenly Father:
I'm praying to you in faith,
to please reveal to her this day.
Patient she has been,
A Wonderful Sister, and a
Great Christian Friend,
In Jesus Name I Pray AMEN

Coco

I would love to hear/read your testimony, please email me:

Lovelylisa79@aol.com